The Christian Character

Understanding the Ways of the Master

Sam Chukwuka Onyeka

authorHOUSE®

AuthorHouse™
1663 Liberty Drive
Bloomington, IN 47403
www.authorhouse.com
Phone: 1-800-839-8640

First published by AuthorHouse   7/18/2011

ISBN: 978-1-4634-1440-5 (sc)
ISBN: 978-1-4634-1441-2 (e)

Library of Congress Control Number: 2011910010

Printed in the United States of America

Any people depicted in stock imagery provided by Thinkstock are models, and such images are being used for illustrative purposes only. Certain stock imagery © Thinkstock.

This book is printed on acid-free paper.

Because of the dynamic nature of the Internet, any web addresses or links contained in this book may have changed since publication and may no longer be valid. The views expressed in this work are solely those of the author and do not necessarily reflect the views of the publisher, and the publisher hereby disclaims any responsibility for them.

Contents

· · · · · · · ·

Preface   vii

Introduction   ix

What is Christian Character?   ix

Humility   1

Love   5

Faith   11

Long-Suffering   15

Truth   19

Goodness   23

Peace   27

Boldness   31

Thanksgiving   35

Forgiveness   37

Holiness   39

Sacrifice   43

Obedience   47

Power   49

Joy   53

Grace   55

Preface

· · · · · · ·

The bountiful love of Jesus Christ is within your reach. Being initiated into the spiritual family of God is only your first step. Now you can fully embrace the knowledge of God and embark on a new and evolving relationship.

By divine election, I was born into a humble family of the Christian faith and raised in the strictest discipline of that faith. Growing up as a child, I enjoyed a good conscience and trusted God for everything, even without any clear understanding of the basis for this trust. In return, I constantly experienced God's mercies and helps.

At adulthood, I questioned a few things my parents had led me to believe, as a basis for developing my own strong personal philosophy of life. In doing this, however, I dabbled in philosophy and also practiced some mysticism. I remained a Christian, but my focus shifted from attaining a close personal relationship with God to seeking after power and financial success. I had reasoned that I could postpone further personal relationship with God until a time when I had become rich and successful.

But I was wrong. I discovered to my chagrin that the more I pursued power and financial success, the more I was enveloped by a thick sense of insecurity and lack. I failed to realize that I was indeed a custodian of

God's infinite creative power: that all I needed was godly inspiration to unlock and release my limitless potential.

This spiritual ignorance held me in bondage for several years and greatly limited my capacity to fulfill my purpose in life. To say the least, I tended toward failure, despite my appreciable level of education and skills. In consequence, I suffered severe stress for fear of dying young and unfulfilled. This experience continued for years unabated and was actually driving me to the precipice of self-destruction, when suddenly I was recovered by the mercies of the Almighty.

I returned to the knowledge of the only wise God with a resolve to dwell on His Word until my personality was lost in Him. Today, through the revelation of God, I have not only been redirected to success but also freed from all manner of stress, happily fulfilling my purpose in life. This is the story of the divine transformation that altered the entire trajectory of my life.

This book has become an encapsulation of the series of revelations I received from the Word of God. It is aimed at inspiring young and old Christians alike into a desire for an evolving relationship with God.

Kingdom authority is rooted in the character of God and exercisable only by those in higher relationship with Him. You will find spotlighted in this book some godly attributes that you are encouraged to cultivate. To aid quick cultivation, some inspirational tips have been provided at the end of each chapter.

Since my ambition in this book is to reach a diverse audience and not necessarily to be rigorous, I have endeavored—although not at the expense of clarity—to avoid copious referencing and detailed analytical approaches as ought to be the case with a strictly academic text.

Also, as part of my efforts to make the book both informative and readable, I have indented direct quotations from the Scriptures, while references have been confined to the end of the book. All scriptural references are from the King James Version.

The periods of gathering materials and the actual writing of this book have been wonderful time spent with the Holy Spirit, to whom I dedicate this book.

Sam Chukwuka Onyeka
25 February 2011

Introduction

· · · · · · · · · · ·

What is Christian Character?

In simple language, Christian character represents the moral behavioral pattern of the Christian that is consistent with God's nature as exemplified by the life of Jesus Christ and revealed in the Scriptures. This definition assumes that the reader is already a Christian and has a working understanding of the Scriptures. However, for emphasis and for the benefit of those who are yet to be converted into Christianity, it may be necessary to explain the concept further.

It appears to me that many people who claim to be Christians today are confused as to the meaning and essence of Christianity. In this felt confusion, some have seen Christianity as a matter of subscription, while others have considered it an inheritable status, and hence sometimes we hear people talk about having a Christian background. Such conceptions as these miss the point. Clearly, Christianity does not emerge from an individual's background, and it is never a matter for subscription. It is certain, for example, that no one can be a lawyer merely on account of his parents having been lawyers. Likewise, no one can be a Christian merely on account of his parents having been Christians. Also, regular attendance at church services cannot alone make anyone a Christian. To become a Christian, one must be formally enrolled into the family of God.

A Christian is therefore a man or woman who has the nature of Jesus Christ and, by extension, the nature of God. Although flesh and blood, the individual carries the Spirit of God in him. He is therefore able to live above sin. He has authority over the powers of darkness, and the grace of God is ever with him. As a living abode of the Spirit of God, he reflects the nature of God without difficulties.

Practically, Christianity is a state of being. It is the state of being like Jesus Christ. Historically, the idea of Christianity emanated from Antioch. The disciples were called Christians because they behaved like their Master, Jesus Christ. Who then is this man Jesus, and how peculiar is His character?

Jesus Christ, the Son, is a Spirit. He was made in the image and likeness of God the Father. Being the firstborn of all creation, He was in the beginning, and He made all things. By immaculate conception, Jesus was made man. He was therefore a fascinating combination of the Spirit of God and a human body. He thus became the domain of godly power and authority, a conductor of supernatural influence, and an epitome of perfection. Remarkably, this complex nature was the basis for the success of the finished work of redemption.

It takes a great deal of faith in God to practice Christianity. In technical terms, it involves dying to self and becoming recreated in God. It requires establishing a personal relationship with God the Father through faith in the sacrificial death of Jesus Christ, the Son, on the cross of Calvary. A Christian is a regenerate being—a man or woman with the mind of Christ. While living physically on earth, the Christian is empowered to enjoy all the benefits of the kingdom of God.[1]

Having provided basic insight into Christianity, I will now attempt to explain the sister concept: character. Character is the moral strength of an individual or the particular combination of qualities that make someone a particular type of person.[2] Character may also represent a complex of individual disposition toward external realities, influenced by values and idiosyncrasies. It derives from innate values, motives, and the range of choices the individual has imbibed at the various stages of growth and deployed for the purpose of personal relevance. To a large extent, character may be influenced by family values and traits inherited from parents.

Character may be equally translated as the test of will that separates the values of good or bad preference in our actions and inactions. It may reflect the innate strength of the individual disposition that determines the shape of our belief system; the colour of our attitudes, conduct, and feelings; and the weather of our perception. Like a compass, character defines the meaning we give to our impulses, emotions, aspirations, and imaginations.

In reality, we are all born with disposition, but we make our character from the complex choices available to us; hence, as a rule, our disposition influences our character.

The Need for Christian Character

Character is inevitable for every Christian. It is generally what marks him out from the world and is the basis for his enjoying continued relationship with God.[3] God is holy and cannot afford a relationship with an individual that is devoid of character.[4] Anyone who desires close relationship with God must endeavour to depart from evil. I have an assurance that when a Christian is lacking in character, he becomes temporarily separated from God. He quits reflecting the light of God and thereby becomes vulnerable to demonic influences and attacks.

More than being a platform for security, Christian character is important to Christians as a responsibility. Jesus declared categorically to His disciples that they were the salt of the earth and the light of the world.[5]. What an enormous responsibility we have as Christians! Salt can be used for seasoning and also for cleansing. Christians therefore have a responsibility to dignify and not pollute their environment. This means that their conduct at all times must be above board. It is desirable that a Christian should be irreprehensible, endeavoring at all times to bring glory and not shame to the name of our Lord Jesus Christ.

Christians also represent light unto their environment. Accordingly, they must show the way at all times. Apart from being the moral compass of the world, Christians must be pacesetters. They must blaze the trail. Such Christians that cannot affect their environment are practically useless. They are like the salt that has lost its taste in Jesus' example and therefore is good for nothing but to be thrown out and marched under the feet of men. The value of every Christian is the content of his character; hence, he must guard it jealously.

Sources of Christian Character

Christian character is derivable from God's Word and through reflections on the life of Jesus Christ and some faithfully devoted men and women of God.

A fundamental source of Christian character is the Word of God, which reveals God's nature. In the Old Testament, we find some godly attributes directly proclaimed by God personally. When God revealed Himself to Moses in the account of Exodus 34:6–7, He proclaimed some of these attributes:

The Lord, the Lord God, merciful and gracious, longsuffering and abundant in goodness and truth, keeping mercy for thousands, forgiving iniquity and transgression and sin …

From the passage, we identify mercifulness, long-suffering, goodness, truthfulness, and forgiveness as among the divine attributes of God. The New Testament Scriptures clearly spell out the fruit of the Holy Spirit as love, joy, peace, long-suffering, gentleness, faith, meekness, and temperance.[6]

Beyond the above attributes of God that are clearly spelt out, God is constantly reflecting His attributes. In the life of Jesus Christ, we find several dozens of godly attributes: meekness, compassion, self-denial, prudence, faith, love, teaching, help, prayerfulness, consistency, forgiveness, patience, confidence, boldness, obedience, diligence, time-consciousness, honesty, justice, truthfulness, peacefulness, gratitude, etc. We also elicit godly attributes from the lives of several men and women who have served and are serving God faithfully.

Christian Character and Mind Renewal

The mind may be considered the most amazingly complex, and perhaps the most powerful, of all the components of the human creature. It truly evidences the fact that God made man in His image and likeness.[7] Apart from being the control centre of life, the mind also serves as the storehouse of experience and learned values. As well, it is the producer of the mechanism that defines and shapes our thoughts, imaginations, instincts, aspirations, and values, among other competing infrastructure in the consciousness.[8]

The mind establishes the strength of our reasoning, creates and resolves conflicts, and directs our choices, decisions, and judgments from the myriad of options available to us every second of our lives. It controls our conscious and unconscious drives and acts as the pathfinder of our mental direction. The mind sets out our plans and pries into the future with an imagination that is unlimited. The mind makes us do what we do. The mind is consequently the abode of our character.[9]

Salvation, the experience frequently referred to as being born again, is indeed a thing of the mind.[10] It takes place in the mind. It marks a transformation from one level of existence to another, a lifting from the world of carnality into the world of the spirit where men live like God. Following this quiet but automatic transformation, it is desirable that the individual concerned should have his mind renewed.

The need for mind renewal may be apparent from the following example. Imagine yourself as having left your environment with a decision to live permanently in another environment that speaks an entirely different language. In this new environment, you will discover that your former language skills are of no real value to you. Of course, you will need to begin afresh to learn the new language if you must communicate and get on freely in your new environment. Except you are able to learn the new language, you would soon begin to feel a sense of frustration and might consider returning to your former environment with which you were very familiar.

Similarly, the newly born Christian must quickly change his thinking pattern—what one might call his mentality—in order to be able to align himself properly into his new life in Christianity. If otherwise is the case, then he would sooner than later become frustrated and eventually return to his old lifestyle of unrighteousness.

Until one is born again, he holds the mind of the world—that is, the carnal mind. The carnal mind is attached to the world. It is consequently sensuous, doubtful, selfish, and often negative. It generally represents death.[11] In contrast, the Spirit of God powers the mind of God. It is consequently limitless, immortal, positive, strong, and faithful. The mind that is connected to the Spirit of God stays with God. It therefore thinks and behaves like God. It lives.

While living carnally, man has perfected the use of the senses. In the spiritual world, however, those senses are simply a liability. Christians must therefore quickly develop spiritual qualities that can help them adapt to their new spiritual environment. The sooner these qualities are developed, the faster the individual Christian can make spiritual progress, and the more relevant he becomes in the kingdom of God. Conversely, the more the individual Christian neglects to develop these qualities, the more frustrating he finds his new spiritual environment. Hence, it would have been more profitable if he had not been born again, although we already know what fate awaits those who are not born again.

To renew the mind[12] means to deemphasize materialism and to emphasize spirituality. It means overcoming the senses and attaining spiritual insight. It is the same thing as diminishing in the consciousness of physical realities and thinking in terms of creation as a whole. Mind renewal requires abandoning the narrow confines of personal interest and thinking in the interest of humanity as a whole. It means to stop existing and to start living. This power of holistic conception distinguishes man from beasts.

I have discovered that most people practice evil because they are unable to see beyond the base: they are unable to lift their minds from carnality to purposefulness. For instance, I am convinced that if through revelation we realized the real purpose of sex in marriage, we would never engage ourselves in adultery and fornication. Also, when it dawns on us that the Creator made the earth for our enjoyment and has limitless capacity to provide for all of us, then we would have no need for greed and avarice. And when we come to terms with the reality that the basis for divine promotion is humility, we would have no choice but to be humble.

The beauty of mind renewal is that it puts us in the class of God. We become gods by association.[13] Operating with the mind of God enables us to attain even greater heights in the physical, frequently to the amazement of our contemporaries. The explanation for this is that the spiritual realm controls the physical. Thus, Christians live in the physical, yet they live more in the spirit. In this sense, they have conquered the world.

Christian character is inevitable for every Christian; it is not only vital for continued relationship with God but is also a necessary condition for maximizing the benefits of God's kingdom. Christianity is a race, and the secret for success is in understanding the rules. A Christian who cannot reflect Christian character cannot please God and, therefore, is not relevant in God's scheme. To attain eternal life, a Christian must perfect his Christianity through the knowledge of God and Christ.

This knowledge of God—from the point of view of His attributes—is what I have partly presented in this book. A Christian demonstrates his preparedness to receive this all-important knowledge by his total abandonment to God. When he has done that, the Holy Spirit will automatically begin to release knowledge to him through revelations from the Scriptures. Even then, the extent of understanding he may obtain from this revelation is very much dependent on the amount of time and effort he is prepared to invest into searching the Scriptures and meditating on the Word of God. It becomes evident, therefore, that while salvation may be free, eternal life has a price tag. This price tag is abandonment to God and remaining with the Word until you get soaked in it.

With this consciousness, I invite you to embrace Christian character today. You can do this by yielding completely to God, and then making it your utmost desire to know Him deeply by discovering and reflecting on His particular character qualities. In this book, I have spotlighted a few of them, beginning with humility.

Chapter One:
· · · · · · · · · · · ·

Humility

Humble yourselves therefore under the mighty hand of God that he may exalt you in due time.[1]

A modern example of someone who attained greatness through humility is President Goodluck Jonathan of Nigeria. His humble disposition and exemplary sense of loyalty while serving as Deputy Governor of Bayelsa State endeared him to many Nigerians and, in particular, President Olusegun Obasanjo, who without reservation recommended him for a joint presidential ticket with late President Umaru Musa Yar'Adua in 2007. When President Yar'Adua died in office in 2010, Goodluck Jonathan became President of Nigeria without contesting election. Sounds like a fairy tale? Yes. But that's exactly what happened.

I perceive humility to be the state of complete absence of pride in an individual, a state of loss of self. To be humble, therefore, is to surrender completely to the will of God. When we surrender ourselves to the will of God, we become free indeed. This is ironic but true. Indeed, the self is the greatest obstacle to living God's kind of life. Only humility can free us from it. In our relationship with God, we must strive to lose ourselves in Him. The decision to lose or retain it is entirely ours. However, if we truly desire to make spiritual progress, we must lose it. We need the mind of God to excel spiritually.

Humility releases us for use according to the will of God. It is the outward expression of our inward acceptance of God's sovereignty over us. Humility aids us in living as we are, free from all inordinate desire. Humility is the evidence that we understand the principle of collectivism, whereby every bit of creation is vital and working together toward a divine goal. Moreover, it aids us in taking our God-given responsibilities seriously and stirs in us a desire to serve God whole-heartedly.

The Devil lacks humility and therefore cannot lead God's kind of life. Some people think of him as an ugly monster with great horns and a long tail, but we know from the Scriptures[2] that he was an excellent beauty named Lucifer: "the son of the morning star." He was in charge of the heavenly choir until the time he fell. His only problem was pride. The spirit of pride could not allow him to lose himself in God. Today, he is everywhere, pretending to be nice, but ready to press anyone who is not careful into living with pride. Would you let him have his way? God forbid.

Jesus is the direct opposite. His earthly life was humility exemplified. There was no pride found in Him. His personality was totally and completely lost in God, and He was therefore able to declare, "I am in the Father, and the Father in me."[3] Jesus humbled Himself, even to dying on the cross like a common criminal. Appreciating the level of humility in the life of Jesus Christ, the apostle Paul recommended:

> Let this mind be in you, which was also in Christ Jesus: who, being
> in the form of God, thought it not robbery to be equal with God:
> but made Himself of no reputation, and took upon him the form
> of a servant, and was made in the likeness of men:[4]

Rather than aspiring to be equal with God, Jesus humbled Himself and put on the form of man in order that He might fulfill the will of God—namely, to redeem mankind. Thus, Jesus surrendered Himself to be crucified. Paul continued:

> And being found in fashion as a man, he humbled himself, and
> became obedient unto death, even the death of the cross.[5]

Jesus counted the loss of His physical life as nothing compared with fulfilling the will of His Father. He surrendered His will completely in humility. In the spiritual realm, humility brings promotion, just as pride brings demotion. Pride robbed the Devil of his exalted position as music director in heaven and saw him cast down into the earth.[6] Conversely, by humility, Jesus received the ultimate promotion. As Paul concluded:

Wherefore God also hath highly exalted him, and given him a name which is above every name: that at the name of Jesus every knee should bow, of things in heaven, and things in earth, and things under the earth; and that every tongue should confess that Jesus is Lord, to the glory of God the Father.[7]

The earlier we begin to consider ourselves of no reputation, the better for us. Whatsoever little position we occupy, we must resign it to God. He must take the glory for whatever we are and whatever we would be. Always, we must see ourselves as mere privileged servants of God and realize that He could have used any other person as an instrument to perfect His will.

Humility will help us lose confidence in the flesh. It will help us to avoid boasting, and where we must boast at all, we will boast in God. Again, Paul understood this secret when he observed:

For we are the circumcision, which worship God in the Spirit, and rejoice in Christ Jesus, and have no confidence in the flesh.[8]

A Christian who understands the need for the knowledge of Jesus Christ will surrender everything in humility to God. He will cease to think in terms of worldly fame, ungodly riches, and all other forms of earthly pleasure. Like Paul, he will be in a position to declare:

But what things were gain to me, those I counted loss for Christ … That I may know him, and the power of his resurrection, and the fellowship of his sufferings, being conformable unto his death …[9]

Humility will help us to endure suffering for the cause of the gospel without complaining, knowing that suffering is part of the cross and that the suffering of this world cannot compare to the glory that is ahead of us.[10]

Without humility, it becomes difficult to think of brokenness. Yet we must be broken as many times as God will desire to bring us to where He wants us to be. Only by humility can we accept training from God.

Go on living in humility; it is your sure way to spiritual growth.

Tips that can help:

- Make a petition to God every day for the spirit of humility.
- Begin to see the next person as more privileged.

- Be ready to make sacrifices that can win you trust in the future.
- Consider taking up a voluntary assignment in your neighborhood.

Chapter Two:
· · · · · · · · · · ·

Love

That Christ may dwell in your hearts by faith; that ye, being rooted and grounded in love, may be able to comprehend with all saints what is the breadth, and length, and depth, and height; and to know the love of Christ, which passes knowledge, that you might be filled with all the fullness of God.[1]

When the apartheid regime in South Africa came to an end in 1994 and the legendary Nelson Mandela became president of the Republic of South Africa, there was palpable anxiety among the white minority who feared that the black majority under Mandela might consider reprisal actions against them. Contrary to their fears and negative expectations, and with a high sense of love and consideration, Mandela contained the burgeoning racial pressure and successfully united both races into one big family. Today the Republic of South Africa is peaceful and is making steady progress as a nation. What a great lesson in love!

Every Christian should aspire be to be filled with love. Love is the basis for attaining knowledge of God and Christ, which is eternal life.[2] Jesus prayed that His disciples might gain deep understanding of His Father. This request was part of the intercessory prayer He made preparatory to His departure.[3] Paul, the apostle who undoubtedly made the greatest

5

impact in the first century, showed extensive insight into the import of this prayer, even as he strived relentlessly to attain the ultimate knowledge of God. The following are his exact words:

> But what things were gain to me, those I counted loss for Christ. Yet doubtless, and I count all things but loss for the excellency of the knowledge of Christ Jesus my Lord: for whom I have suffered the loss of all things, and do count them but dung, that I may win Christ …That I may know him, and the power of his resurrection, and the fellowship of his sufferings, being made conformable unto his death.[4]

From the account of the Scriptures, there could be three steps to attaining ultimate knowledge of God. First, the person receives Jesus Christ into his life by faith. Next, he becomes rooted and grounded in love. Then he begins to comprehend along with the saints the deep things of God, which in its fullness translates to eternal life. This is exactly what Paul was labouring to explain to the church at Ephesus. The focus here, however, is on love. I will therefore proceed to explain the meaning of love and as much as possible explain the means of becoming rooted and grounded in it.

Love, simply put, is the affection that brings pleasure. It could also represent wholesome attachment or dedication to someone or something. I see love as a natural feeling that emanates from the spirit-man and receives physical expression by the operation of the mind. I perceive the human heart as the storehouse of the spirit-man and the mind as a psycho-spiritual abstraction that links the spirit to the body. The mind can easily represent the centre of life itself in such a way that whatsoever enters the mind ultimately gets to the spirit-man and whatsoever comes from the spirit-man passes through the mind to the body. No wonder the Scriptures insist that the mind be guarded with diligence.[5]

God's love is spiritual; hence it would be difficult for anyone to reflect the love of God without having to surrender to the Spirit of God. The prescription for reflecting God's love is therefore to surrender completely to God. It does not require physical effort. No one should struggle to love. When the Spirit of God is in an individual, he unconsciously begins to reflect God's love. However, attracting and retaining the Spirit of God requires sanctification.

Love is no doubt the greatest and the strongest character quality of the Christian. It is an invaluable instrument in the service of God. Love is particularly relevant to the Christian because it is commanded.[6] As a matter of obligation, we are to love God as well as our fellow men. Jesus charged His disciples on love as follows.

This is my commandment, that you love one another, as I have loved you.[7]

It is always difficult to resist the temptation to limit our show of love to people in the household of God. But love is whole and not segregated. When one has the Holy Spirit in him, he feels the need to love even his enemies. He has compassion toward them because the Holy Spirit would have already revealed to him their fate. He would therefore desire their genuine repentance and salvation. We have great lessons to learn in this direction from the examples of Jesus Christ and the apostle Stephen. Both prayed for forgiveness on behalf of their persecutors and executioners. The loss of their physical lives could not compare to their joy in realizing that God had forgiven their enemies. This is clearly in line with God's purpose for humankind. God does not enjoy the death of the wicked, but His earnest desire is that all should come to repentance.[8]

Although there are several Greek words for love, the New Testament uses only two words for love: agape and philia.[9] Agape love is one-directional love. It is selfless love, the type of love that God has for us that prompted Him to sacrifice His only begotten son. Agape love is also the type of love that Jesus showed us when He abandoned His privileged position in heaven to suffer shame, humiliation, and death at the cross of Calvary. Agape love is pure and perfect love. No one who shows agape love will do anything that may offend God.

On the contrary, philia love can be two-sided, incomplete, selfish, and never flowing steadily. Many Christians today have preferred to show this type of love to God. They desire to follow the Master but cannot bear to surrender their desires and ambition to Him. I make bold to state that none who show only the philia kind of love can acquire full knowledge of God.

Our level of understanding of God and Jesus Christ is a product of the depth of love we have for both; for it is impossible to acquire deep knowledge of one that we do not truly love and desire. We find many today that profess Christianity yet crave power and affluence, even at the risk of offending God. They wish to go out there to get what they want and then return to God. Such people's commitment is, to say the least, predicated on their ulterior motives. In a sense, they will remain committed to God for as long as God blesses them with their hearts' desires.

Agape love will move us to serve God without expectations. Christians with this kind of love would remain committed whether or not things are working out for them. You will find them remaining focused, deploying their God-given talents toward finding solutions to the common challenges of mankind. Their only preoccupation is to fulfill their purpose in life. Christians have no reason to be separated from the love of God. Instead, they should remain and grow in it. To grow in the love of God means we must let our relationship with God become an obsession.

It is also important for Christians to realize that sometimes adversity can be a test of love. This has always been the case and will never change for any particular individual. Only a positive attitude can see us through. Job was a remarkable example in this regard. At the height of His pain, His attitude toward God did not change. He was therefore able to declare:

Though he slay me, yet will I trust in him ...[10]

Similarly, there is need to avoid the misconception that when we surrender to God our lives will be all prosperity, divine health, and so on. Of course, God's desire for us is that we prosper and be in good health. However, if we sincerely desire to grow spiritually, we must accept that union with God requires crucifixion in many respects, and that crucifixion is the basis for obedience. If it were not, the Scriptures would not have recorded this:

Though He were a Son, yet learned he obedience by the things
which he suffered. And being made perfect, he became the author
of eternal salvation unto all them that obey him.[11]

Jesus is God, but having taken the form of man, it was inevitable that He subdue human tendencies and attain perfection while still human. This is the reason He had to pass through some tests. When we have come into a relationship with God by grace, we need to attain perfection in order to blend with Him. Perfection requires that we pass through extensive purging, which is only achievable through trials. As humans, we regard trials as sufferings. Love for God will make us accept these trials in good faith. The Holy Spirit gave this understanding to the wise king Solomon, and he wrote:

In the day of prosperity be joyful, but in the day of adversity
consider: God also hath set the one over against the other to the
end that man should find nothing after him.[12]

James the apostle operated with a similar mind-set when he admonished:

My brethren, count it all joy when you fall into diverse temptations; Knowing that the trying of your faith worketh patience. But let patience have her perfect work, that you may be perfect and entire, wanting nothing.[13]

You will never be able to find comfort from men any time you are passing through hardship occasioned by a test for perfection. Any comfort that there may be comes from the Lord and from Him alone.

Let your love for God continue to grow in bounds and become enduring.

Tips that can help:

- Begin to think about what you can do to please God on a daily basis.
- Learn more about God's love by reading a portion of the Scriptures daily.
- Always ask God in prayer to fill you with His Spirit of love.
- Identify at least one person in your vicinity with urgent need of assistance, and render what help you can.

Chapter Three:

Faith

*And Jesus answering saith unto them, "Have faith in God.
For verily, I say unto you, That whosoever shall say to this
mountain, Be thou removed, and be thou cast into the
sea; and shall not doubt in his heart, but shall believe that
those things which he saith shall come to pass; he shall have
whatsoever he saith."[1]*

A couple I know suffered barrenness for a long time. Following a complicated
health challenge, the woman had her entire womb removed by surgical
operation. Thereafter, doctors confirmed to the couple that medically
they would never be able to have their own biological children. The couple
later became pastors in a big church in Nigeria. Their commitment to
the kingdom of God provoked a family relationship between them and
the presiding bishop of the church, who on one occasion prophesied
fruitfulness unto them.

The couple exercised strong faith in the Word of God and the counsel
of the servant of God. They trusted God in spite of their knowledge of
the prevailing medical condition. Exactly nine months after the prophesy,
the woman was delivered of a bouncing baby boy. The story is not ended.
After a couple of years, the woman conceived again and delivered a baby

girl. The children are now adults, and the couple have continued to be an inspiration to many who are trusting God for the fruit of the womb.

People exercise faith on a daily basis, sometimes without knowing it. For instance, you sit on a particular chair because you trust and, by implication, exercise faith in the ability of the chair to sustain your weight and not knock you over. You take a step and begin to walk because you have faith in the ability of your legs to carry you. You enter an aircraft and relax in your seat because you have confidence in the ability of the pilot and the competence and expertise of the manufacturers. In each of these examples, it is more likely that you will decline any steps where you have doubts. It is therefore evident that doubt prevents you from taking steps, while faith moves you into taking action, the two being in opposition.

In the physical, actions are based on mental judgments, influenced by senses and perceptions. However, in the spiritual realm, faith directs every action. This is so because, while the physical senses are limited by time and space, the spiritual realm is unimaginably extensive and without limits. You will only be able to appreciate what I am labouring to explain if you have entered an aircraft or a submarine. You no doubt have noticed that the coast is so expansive that the pilot does not rely on his natural senses but on a pair of compasses to pick his direction.

Similarly, you can never imagine the size of the spirit realm and still think that your physical eyes could be of any practical value. Movement and other activities in the spiritual realm are possible only by faith. Man is a spirit that lives in a body. He is only having an experience in the earth's physical environment. He came from the spirit realm and resides here as a pilgrim. Man is like an astronaut on a visit to the moon who, upon accomplishing his assignment, returns to his base.

The capacity to exercise faith is inherent in man. God originally planted it in his spirit. It is this faith that enables man to receive salvation. It should be noted however, that the unregenerate person is detached from the spirit of God; hence he cannot exercise God's kind of faith. He relies on his intellect with the result that each time he is unable to rationalize anything, he refrains from taking steps on it. On the contrary, the regenerate person has his spirit connected to God's spirit. Consequently, he can easily exercise God's kind of faith. He becomes fully conscious of himself. Although he lives on earth for the purpose before stated, he nevertheless understands the spiritual realm—particularly as it relates to how to move and survive in it. He learns faith as the language of the spirit.

To become regenerate, one must accept that God inhabits and controls the spiritual realm. Next, he must believe in his heart and acknowledge with his mouth that Jesus Christ is the Son of God and that He died and resurrected on the third day. Christians must realize the need to appropriate and exercise their faith.[2] A non-appropriated gift remains the property of the giver. Before we go into explaining the extent to which a Christian can go in appropriating and/or exercising his faith, let us explore further the concept of faith.

To have faith is to believe in something without really demanding evidence.[3] When there is faith, it means there is absolute trust and confidence in what one has chosen to explore. It is evident, therefore, that those lacking faith cannot trust and may never care whether they are trusted. Faithful people develop a sense of character and live a purposeful life. They build their lives on principles rather than chance. Faith enables us to work productively toward a desired goal. It attracts the spirit of resilience and industry that are vital for manifestation on earth.

Faith has a necessary relationship with humility. It is evident that without humility it will be difficult to develop an open mind to the extent that we can rely on something we have not seen or cannot see. We can hardly experience the desire to seek after God until we have strong faith in His existence. Neither can we please God in the absence of faith.[4] It is strong faith in His existence that puts us in the class of God and makes us live like Him. Faith is the character of God, His territory, and His language. Many Christians today are sinking in the ocean of life because that vital life jacket—faith—is lacking. Jesus said, If you can believe, all things are possible to him who believes.[5] Yet not a few things are impossible for most Christians. The ability to exercise faith is what guarantees your place in destiny.

I will now return to explain the means by which faith can be developed and perfected. You will almost certainly agree that a newly born baby that is not fed constantly will invariably grow weak and, in the extreme case, die. The situation is no different with faith. The seed of faith planted in you at birth germinates at the point you became born again. You therefore need to feed it constantly with the Word of God. The Word of God is food for our faith. We must eat it constantly. Learning about God through the Scriptures reinforces the faith God has deposited in us and renews our minds. More emphatically, the Scriptures say that faith comes by hearing the Word of God.[6] It is God's desire that we transform our lives and redirect our courses to follow His own paths.

Apart from feeding our faith, we must take time to exercise it. In the eleventh chapter of the book of Hebrews, we are treated with a long list of men and women who accomplished great and extraordinary feats in their service to God because of their faith. These exercised their faith by accepting challenges in their hands. You can exercise your faith by accepting challenges without complaining. This is key, as God will invariably try our faith and we must prove our faith before He can use us to accomplish great things concerning His purpose.[7]

Another critical aspect in developing faith is work. Faith is worthless without works. Simply put, faith must be in operation. It must be practically evident. James therefore wrote:

> What doth it profit, my brethren, though a man say he hath faith, and have not works? Can faith save him? ... Even so faith, if it hath not works, is dead, being alone.[8]

Except we are able to match faith with works, we may never be able to move toward God's desired direction for our life. Seeking after God and surrendering to him requires a great deal of work. Christian character is effective only when we can match faith with good works.

Stabilize your faith by accepting the challenges of life in good faith and considering trials as opportunities for attaining greater spiritual heights and obtaining the ultimate reward. Always realize that:

> Blessed is the man who endures temptation; for when he has been approved, he will receive the crown of life, which the Lord has promised to those who love Him.[9]

Tips that can help:

- Pray regularly for the Spirit of faith.
- Read the Word of God daily.
- Match your faith with actions.
- Think positively about every challenge.

Chapter Four:
. . . .

Long-Suffering

The Lord is not slack concerning his promise, as some count slackness, but is longsuffering to us-ward, not willing that any should perish, but that all should come to repentance.[1]

An evangelist lost all four of his children in an accident while traveling to a crusade venue. He did not postpone the crusade. Instead, on that same night of the road tragedy, he ministered his best sermon, being filled by the power of God. Many repented and were delivered from yokes and bondages. On the morning of the next day, arrangements were made to recover the corpses for burial. The evangelist did not stop because of the experience, neither did he question God about it. Some years later, God, through the same woman, gave the evangelist four other extraordinary children. Today he still preaches the gospel, with signs and wonders following. What a practical demonstration of long-suffering!

In the preceding section, we noted that faith in God would help us endure challenges, knowing that they are inevitable for the proper development of our spirituality. Now, the ability to sustain hardship or pain for a reasonably long time without complaining or murmuring is called long-suffering. It is a character quality and also a great attribute of God.[2] He exemplifies this in His patience toward humanity, and it flows from His genuine desire for all to attain repentance. No doubt, God is hurting each time we commit sin, yet He is never in a hurry to invoke His coercive power of discipline against us. All He does is hide His face and literally withdraw His divine presence from us. The aim is to preserve us from destruction, for God is a "consuming fire."

Jesus showed an example of long-suffering by physically dying on the cross of Calvary. He was whipped, stabbed, abused, and finally crucified. Just consider the extent of pain He suffered for your sake and mine. A remarkable thing about Jesus' experience is that he passed through the suffering without complaining. In his prophetic account of Jesus' experience, Isaiah observed:

> He was oppressed and he was afflicted, yet he opened not his mouth: he is brought as a lamb to the slaughter, and as a sheep before her shearers is dumb, so he openeth not his mouth.[3]

Long-suffering made it possible for Jesus to attain obedience and, consequently, the perfection that made him the author of eternal salvation to all who obey Him.[4]

Remembering what He had to pass through on our behalf, Jesus is hurting each time we return to sin. Yet He does not cease from advocating on our behalf before His Father. If we desire to be one in God like Jesus Christ, we must embrace long-suffering.

In particular, long-suffering entails that we forgive others as frequently as they may put us into physical or emotional hardship. It equally requires that we forgive ourselves each time we make a mistake and each time we find ourselves going astray.

Long-suffering is essential in managing brokenness, which is inevitable in attaining spiritual heights. The reality remains that God must first break us in order that He might remold us into the form He wants us to be. He will break us as many times as it may become necessary according to His taste and desire for us. Through long-suffering, we are in a position to accept whatever discipline the Lord may chose to bring upon us.

Sometimes, long-suffering might be the means of testing our love for God. We must therefore learn to endure hardship with patience and hope. God may frequently permit severe hardship into your life. Do not regard this as a mistake. It is His doing. Learn to bear all that happen to you, even in confusion. Avoid insisting on figuring it out, and be willing to surrender your right to ask why.

Again, it takes long-suffering to build faith. Sometimes you find that after you have approached God with a request, you receive no help. While you wait the problem persists. The lesson, therefore, is that between the prayer and the answer, you are building faith. You only need to stand and wait.

Again, in relation to receiving the gifts of God, you need long-suffering. Remember, the gifts are not always there just for the asking. You need to pray and travail for it. You equally need to wait patiently upon God. Anyone who finds it difficult to take pains and to wait patiently is certainly not a candidate for the gifts of God.

Finally, long-suffering will move you to have pity for others. It makes you put yourself in their shoes all the time. It equally helps you develop the necessary compassion required for the working of miracles. You already know how waiting feels, and therefore you appreciate the need to pray insistently for such people.

Tips that can help:

- Pray each day for the spirit of long-suffering.
- Identify a character in the Scriptures who showed long-suffering, and meditate on his experience.
- Make a decision to trust God, regardless of your present experience.
- Identify someone in your neighborhood who is going through a trial of faith, and encourage him.

Chapter Five:
· · · · · · · · · · ·

Truth

Sanctify them through thy truth: thy word is truth.[1]

Today, many people are suffering as a result of atrocities of the past. I know some people who once lived their lives swindling others. In their heydays, they commanded much financial power and influence. But today they live as old, poor fools. Their names stink. They live in regret, having destroyed that most valuable asset in life—a good reputation. Even their children are not spared. They too carry the burden of a bad family name. Who says it does not pay to live a life of truthfulness?

Truthfulness is a character quality expected of every Christian. It is the quality of being able to identify with the truth always, without wavering. But what exactly is the truth?

In the history of philosophy, the concept of truth developed from the Greek word alethia meaning "uncovered." In the course of time, however, truth became associated with the Latin word veritas, meaning "certainty of representational thought." Truth, in the everyday use of the concept, was a process of knowing more and more about a thing, meaning that the truth about the object of knowledge has to do with what we can say has become unconcealed or revealed about it.

With medieval philosophy, truth developed into adequacio intellectus et rei, meaning "conformity of the intellect with the object." Accordingly, truth became a datum instead of a dialectical process, dictating more attention for the thought than the reality that gave rise to it. This is the parting point between the philosophical concept of truth and the revealed truth of God.[2]

I have tried hard to resist the temptation to be drawn into philosophical arguments in this book. The primary reason for this is my conviction that it takes more than academic learning and philosophical disputation to arrive at knowledge. Moreover, no one can deny that the things we hold with the greatest certainty are those lessons we have learnt through experience.

The Scriptures reveal only one truth, and that is the Word of God. The Word of God is the Word of Truth. Hence, it is written:

> Of his own will begat he us with the word of truth, that we should be a kind of firstfruits of his creatures.[3]

Jesus Christ is the embodiment of truth, and it is difficult for anyone to live truthfully without having the life of Jesus Christ in him. As human, Jesus lived a life of truthfulness because He had the Father, who cannot lie in Him. Jesus is the Truth and also the Way and Life.[4] It is therefore opposite of Christian character to lie. No wonder the Devil is called the father of all lies. He lied from the beginning and still lies today. Any Christian that lies is loyal only to the Devil and cannot represent God.

If anything, lying provokes the Spirit of God. God is omniscient and therefore knows the truth about all things. It will therefore amount to insulting the sensibility of the Supreme Intelligence to lie at all. It is even worse when it pertains to things of the Spirit. This is the reason the Holy Spirit struck down Ananias and his wife Sapphira when they lied concerning the amount of money for which they sold their property.[5] Many Christians today take advantage of the so-called "dispensation of grace" to insult and annoy God. They lie even in circumstances where lying is uncalled-for. The Bible commands: "But let your communication be yea, yea; Nay, nay: for whatsoever is more than these cometh of evil."[6]

Truthfulness strengthens our conscience, gives us inner peace, and makes us feel a sense of boldness. A truthful person is not only factual but also reliable. Truth is the foundation of moral discipline and success. It is the bedrock of spiritual security and social responsibility. Any inclination toward rewarding values is traceable to truth. There is no alternative to truth for anyone desiring spiritual growth.

Lying is a breach of ethical values, contempt for moral responsibility, and disregard for God. Liars lack discipline in them. Therefore, they frequently resort to sensuous living that robs them of spiritual balance. Lying can easily become a way of life. Thus, the individual lies even to himself, covering up problems and pretending they do not exist—including a problem with lying. Whether we like it or not, someday we must face the reality and experience the pain and anguish caused by our lies.

Telling the truth always creates in us a sense of confidence, purposefulness, and value-consciousness. It kindles in us a ceaseless desire to pursue divine goals and meaningful preoccupations. It helps us remain in good relationship with God during and after our earthly life.

To enjoy the life of truthfulness, we need humility and contentment. Those who cannot overcome greed and avarice cannot live a life of truthfulness. Lack of contentment pushes the victim to detest his standing in life on a daily basis. It makes him feel that he is someone else, without regard for spiritual and moral consequences. Lying can only earn you temporary advantage; it can never give you a lasting benefit.

On a final note, may I recall for you the words of the Psalmist:

What man is he that desireth life, and loveth many days, that he may see good? Keep thy tongue from evil, and thy lips from speaking guile.[7]

Tips that can help:

- Pray always for the spirit of truth.
- Make a decision to always identify with the truth, not minding the present cost.
- Make friends with those who will stand for the truth always.

Chapter Six:

· · · · · · · · · · ·

Goodness

A good man out of the good treasure of the heart bringeth forth good things: and an evil man out of the evil treasure bringeth forth evil things.[1]

Humans have free will. By this I mean that every individual has the right to make decisions freely without any undue influence. This right to self-determination is otherwise referred to as freedom of choice. Consequently, each person has the right to live as he pleases. However, God in His wisdom has laid the foundation of the universe upon immutable principles. One of the most fundamental of those principles is that you reap what you sow. God is so particular about this principle of sowing and reaping that the Scriptures counsel:

> Be not deceived; God is not mocked; for whatsoever a man soweth, that shall he also reap.[2]

Accordingly, if a man sows good treasures, he reaps good treasures. If he sows evil, he will likewise reap evil. It also follows that although man has freedom of choice, if he exercises it wrongly, he will surely pay for it.

Our capacity to resolve to do things right and according to the dictates of the Scriptures is the essence of goodness. Goodness is a divine attribute of God. As we have earlier noted, when God manifested Himself to Moses, among the attributes that He revealed was goodness. Goodness is the opposite of evil. It is always evident in good works.

Goodness is a state of being positively resolute. This entails building our lives upon honest intentions. Goodness is rooted in the conviction or determination to do things within acceptable standards, whether ethical, moral, or divine.

To reflect the quality of goodness, we must discipline our minds. We must be constantly in touch with the Spirit of God. The Holy Spirit will guide our thoughts and actions with a sense of goodness when we have resolved to live uprightly.

Goodness is associated with light. This is why God is the Father of all lights.[3] On the contrary, evil works are associated with darkness. Such works are dirty and unhealthy, and no one involved in them can desire light. The evil ones dread light, lest their evil works should become manifest. When we engage in good works, we show that we are children of light, having nothing to hide. Thus, we reflect the light of God, which the Devil cannot comprehend.

Goodness is the basis for freedom from harm. When we live a life of goodness, we attract divine protection. The apostle Peter was so certain of this particular revelation that he asserted:

> And who is he that will harm you if ye be followers of that which is good?[4]

Besides, it takes goodness to receive from the Lord. Anyone who earnestly seeks after goodness will certainly obtain favour from the Lord.[5] When we become committed to good work, we begin to attract God's pleasure, and He blesses and protects us in return.

Goodness should never be sustained by selfish and personal efforts. It takes the grace of God through the Holy Spirit that dwells inside the Christian to reflect goodness. If the motive for a good gesture is not honest, then it becomes self-righteousness. Self-righteousness is offensive to God. Man at his best state cannot stand in the presence of a holy and righteous God. When we are genuinely committed to God, we receive the unction that enables us to attain to good works by the ministry of the Holy Spirit. Goodness will come naturally, without any desire to be self-fulfilled by it.

Tips that can help:

- Pray for divine enablement for consistent good work.
- Resolve always to allow God to take glory from your good works.
- Identify someone in need today, and render assistance to him or her.

Chapter Seven:
. . . .

Peace

Peace I leave with you, my peace I give unto you: not as the world giveth, give I unto you. Let not your heart be troubled, neither let it be afraid.[1]

We now live in a world of instability. Everyone desires peace, but it appears that peace has eluded mankind. Only very few people who are in close relationship with God enjoy peace.

I see peacefulness as the quality of being stable, calm, cool, and serene, without anxiety or worries. It is the ability to remain calm and stable in the face of life-threatening realities. It is, therefore, a state of rest. Those who practice Christianity with commitment are cool, calm, and serene people. They live in a state of freedom from anxiety and stress. Technically speaking, they attain a state of rest. Indeed, it sounds inconceivable for the living to attain perfect peace. But as Christians, we are already dead in Christ Jesus. And having resurrected with Him, we now live, move, and have our being in him.[2]

Christians must learn to be at peace all the time. A fundamental reason for this is that we need to hear from God always. We need His direction and guidance in virtually everything if we are to succeed. We have evidence from the scriptures that God speaks to us from time to time:

The heavens declare the glory of God; and the firmament showeth his handiwork. Day unto day uttereth speech, and night unto night showeth knowledge.[3]

We therefore need to be at peace in order to hear Him. This is particularly important given that the voice of God is a still, small voice,3 and only those who are at peace can hear it. By extension, the more peaceful you are, the more receptive you become to the voice of the Lord, and you will never miss your direction in life. Yes, we have divine assurance of direction:

And thine ears shall hear a word behind thee, saying, This is the way, walk in it.[4]

It is reassuring to realize that Christians need not struggle to attain peace. Already, Jesus Christ is our peace. All we need do is to become soaked with the Word of God that gives us peace.

The earth's physical environment is full of pollution and other distractions, and this makes it difficult for anyone to connect with God. Connecting to the Spirit of God, therefore, requires that we make extra effort to remove ourselves from the noisy and deafening influences of the world. In order to achieve this, we must sincerely desire interaction with God:

Through desire a man, having separated himself, seeketh and intermeddleth with all wisdom.[5]

We enjoy peace when we apply our faith to the Word of God. Peacefulness is evidence of our faith in the Word of God. It is an indication that we realize that God is in us. In reality, we live, move, and have our being in Him. If we are conscious of our identity in Christ, no life-threatening challenge will be able to throw us into confusion. Like Jesus, we would always know what to do. Jesus demonstrated evidence of unshaken faith and thus remained peaceful when He fell asleep in the face a wild storm that threatened to capsize the boat He was in.

Faith in the Word of God made the three young Hebrew men able to resist the command of Nebuchadnezzar to bow down to worship his idol. They trusted God's Word that:

...when thou walkest through the fire, thou shalt not be burned: neither shall the flame kindle upon thee.[6]

It is faith in the Word that gave Daniel peace while in the lions' den. Daniel seemed to have heard God when He said:

Fear thou not; for I am with thee: be not dismayed; for I am Thy God: I will strengthen thee; yea, I will help thee; I will uphold thee with the right hand of my righteousness.[7]

Faith in the Word of God made Moses calm after the children of Israel had become sandwiched between the Red Sea and Pharaoh's army. He was thus able to declare to the Israelites:

The Lord shall fight for you, and ye shall hold your peace.[8]

In another dimension, one may enjoy peace with God, with self, and with others. Peace with God means that one is saved and living a life of holiness in God. Having peace with God enables us to attain peace within ourselves. Knowledge of God guarantees us the ability to reconcile existential conflicts, and we enjoy peace thereby.

Peace with others arises sometimes out of a sense of freedom from rejection. It means that our friends, colleagues, and associates accept us. Peace with others is not necessarily an indication that we have peace with God. It is more important, however, that we be at peace with God.

Regardless, as much as it depends on him, a Christian should be at peace with all men. Yet seeking peace with all men does not mean we should not feel pain when we are hurt. Rather, it is desirable that we bear the pain with a sense of forgiveness, never thinking of revenge.

In conclusion, the amount of peace you can enjoy at a particular time is a product of the depth you have attained in the Word of God. You certainly have no choice better than to make the Word of God dwell richly in you in all wisdom.[9]

Tips that can help:

- Pray for divine peace.
- Make time each day to meditate on the Word of God.
- Ask for God's forgiveness for every sin that is weighing against your peace.
- Ensure that you forgive everyone who offends you during the course of the day.

Chapter Eight:
. . . .

Boldness

...the righteous are bold as a lion.[1]

Boldness is an attribute of lions. They are never turned back. They are fearless and ready to defend their territory and young ones.

I see boldness as the capacity to step out without fear or doubt as to the outcome. It is self-confidence instigated by knowledge and faith. Boldness is part of the attributes of God. He speaks with boldness and it happens. As the Lion of the tribe of Judah, Jesus is boldness personified. No wonder He was able to lift and open the scroll that no one dared to touch or open.[2] With boldness He confronted principalities and powers and made public show of them and triumphed over them in hell.[3]

There is nothing like having power and being conscious of it. It makes you talk and act with confidence. When you lack power, you tend to be fearful and timid. This is the reason you never find the boldness of princes among slaves. Thank God, for we are kings and priests unto Him,[4] and we have received not the spirit of fear but of boldness and a sound mind.[5]

At new birth, we are let loose from the kingdom of darkness and translated into the kingdom of God. In Christ, we sit in heavenly places, far above principalities and powers.[6] We receive power to trample upon the Devil and his demons. Never let this consciousness depart from you. It is what makes the difference. The Devil is very much aware that he has been defeated and can no longer exercise authority over you. The only legitimate weapon he has is fear. No wonder the Scriptures say that he walks as a roaring lion, seeking whom to devour.[7] His desire is to infuse fear into you and ultimately to strip you of your salvation. Often, he brings us face to face with the challenges of life. However, God is not bothered about this. The reason is that He has already assured us of His support, and indeed His grace is sufficient for us.

Besides, God has given us the Holy Spirit. According to the Scriptures, the Holy Spirit will teach us all things and will bring all things to our remembrance.[8] The Holy Spirit is therefore our primary helper in the search for answers to the issues of life. In practice, the Holy Spirit shows us through the Scriptures how to handle the issues of life. He does this by giving us insights from the Scriptures. When the Holy Spirit sheds light in our hearts by the entrance of the Word, we gain revelation. Revelation is the highest level attainable by mortals for understanding of the Word of God on a particular issue. Through revelation, we can become masters over the affairs of life, and this awareness gives us boldness to confront any challenge that may come our way.

Christians need insight continually. The more revelation we are able to catch, the more competent we become and the more boldly we can confront life's challenges. My personal experience can be a typical example.

As I indicated in the preface to this book, I was held down by ignorance up to the point of failure—until I began to receive insights into God's Word. As I continued to catch more and more revelations, my boldness increased, and I developed confidence to handle challenges. You can do better if only if you can settle down with the Word of God.

Christianity is averse to fear. Fear opens the gate for the Devil to unsettle you and make a mess of the salvation that God through the blood of Jesus Christ delivered to you free of charge. God is sorely pained when we surrender our dominion to the Devil because of fear. He has therefore destined fearful persons for hellfire. That will never be our portion.

As Christians, we have a duty to resist the Devil. We need boldness to resist him. Boldness is an act of faith. If you lack boldness, you will never be able to exercise kingdom power, and this is as good as falling prey to the Devil. Resist the Devil boldly by faith, and he will surely flee from you.

Tips that can help:

- Pray for the spirit of boldness and of a sound mind.

- Resolve never to give up on your challenges.
- Search out the Scriptures for men and women with bold spirits, and follow their paths.

Chapter Nine:
· · · · · · · · · · ·

Thanksgiving

In everything, give thanks: for this is the will of God in Christ Jesus concerning You.[1]

It is a good thing to give thanks. Much more, it is desirable that we develop a mentality of gratitude, regardless of our present circumstances. Someone may ask if it makes sense to give thanks concerning problems and challenges. Taking a closer look at the anchor scripture above, you will discover that it did not say we should give thanks for all situations. It simply says we should be grateful in all situations. We are to give thanks to God in all situations, because we already know that all things work together for the good of them that love God.[2] Regardless of your experience in life, give thanks, for you have victory already.

Understand with the mentality of a child—without the least doubt—that it is impossible for you to be disgraced. When you cultivate the habit of thanking God in all situations, He mobilizes His angels in your favour, and you will certainly live according to His will concerning you. Giving thanks is the opposite of grumbling and murmuring, and in God's sight, murmuring is worse than the sin of witchcraft.[3]

In the course of my relationship with God, I have many times experienced the miracle of thanksgiving. While living as an immigrant in a foreign land, I became so impoverished that I could not afford a pair of shoes to wear. Instead of murmuring, I began to thank God for life and for a future. I also thanked Him for the shoes that I had worn in the past by His help. Almost immediately after that personal thanksgiving session, God miraculously opened up a financial door that took care of my need for a pair of shoes at the time. Thanksgiving shows that we love God and trust Him in every situation. We thereby acknowledge His omnipotence, and He will be eager to strengthen us, even in our challenges.

In the physical, thanksgiving is usually in response to what we have received already. However, sometimes we may prompt help and assistance by giving thanks in advance. For example, when we ask someone for help which he can afford and thank him in advance, we are more likely to receive the help than if we stop at just making the request.

This principle works more in the spiritual realm. In fact, in the spiritual realm, thanksgiving is a condition for receiving. By giving thanks in advance, we exercise faith in the ability of the giver, and we literally call out those things that are not as if they are.[4] Jesus practiced thanksgiving extensively. He thanked God in every situation. He used thanksgiving as a basis for working miracles. His thanksgiving prompted God to grant His request for the resurrection of Lazarus.[5] On that occasion, Jesus was convinced that God would hear him as always. He therefore thanked Him for the particular thing requested and reminded Him of the inevitability of an answer. God surely answered him.

You are unlikely to receive any help from God until you learn to give thanks. Give thanks always for the help already received, but give thanks all the more for the help you are yet to receive. Give thanks for God's manifold blessings, but also remember to give thanks while you are suffering and going through pain. Give thanks in everything.

Tips that can help:

- Pray for the spirit of thanksgiving.
- Give thanks to God for every piece of blessing.
- Do not let a day pass without recounting His helps and giving thanks.
- Thank Him for the challenges you are facing and for the ones you will face in the future.

Chapter Ten:
· · · · · · · · · · ·

Forgiveness

If we confess our sins, he is faithful and just to forgive us our sins and to cleanse us from all unrighteousness.[1]

Forgiveness is an attribute of God. To forgive means to write off our grievances against those who have wronged us or made us feel pain. Often, in the course of our daily lives, we consciously and unconsciously offend others. Others also offend us sometimes. Man is born imperfect. He is always in the struggle to free himself from imperfection. God understands our imperfection and desires that we become perfect. Accordingly, He has given us His grace freely to assist. Yet, while we work hard to attain perfection, we occasionally err. God therefore forgives us freely when we err. He does not call to mind our inadequacies, especially when we have repented and genuinely asked for forgiveness.

For this same reason, Jesus came and died on the cross of Calvary. He came to deliver us from the clutches of sin and death. God through Jesus Christ established that it is possible for humans to live without sin. Consequently, when we forgive others, we imitate God and Jesus Christ. On the contrary, when we fail to forgive, we show that we have no portion in God. Moreover, unforgiveness always develops into a feeling of bitterness and subsequently turns into hatred. We know from the Scriptures that whosoever hates his brother is a murderer.[2]

Forgiving others is one way we can obtain forgiveness from God. Given that we offend God very frequently, it follows that we have a duty to forgive all those who offend us if we expect forgiveness from God. When we cannot forgive those who offend us, there is no way we can expect forgiveness from God. It would amount to God playing a double standard if it were otherwise.

A forgiving person has a humble spirit. He therefore does not puff up but considers others as more privileged. Both Jesus and Stephen exemplified this character quality. They prayed God to forgive their assailants. God is happy with us when we freely forgive others, especially when we are ready to pray for forgiveness on their behalf.

It is important that our forgiveness becomes total. When we forgive others, we must forget the incident too. We must never be in the habit of recalling the sad event or have occasion to remind those who wronged us of how they offended us and how bad we felt. Jesus was a fine example of total and unrelenting forgiveness. Peter denied Him thrice in a few seconds. Yet when Peter repented, Jesus forgave him completely. Jesus confirmed this by assigning to Peter the all-important role of leadership among the disciples.

Sometimes, it might be necessary that we forgive ourselves. Forgiving ourselves when we make a mistake shows that we are humble, and by so doing, we acknowledge our imperfection and our desire to attain perfection. Failure to forgive ourselves is, however, an indication of spiritual arrogance.

God is an example of self-forgiveness. Although He felt grief in His heart and repented that He made man because of man's tendency toward evil, yet He quickly forgave Himself and proceeded with arrangements to redeem man from the clutches of sin and death. That singular decision by God to forgive Himself is the basis for the salvation we now enjoy in Christ. What wonder forgiveness can do!

Endeavour to cultivate the character quality of forgiveness. You will never regret it.

Tips that can help:

- Pray for the spirit of forgiveness.
- Make a decision to forgive all who have offended you in the past.
- Never go to sleep with bitterness against anyone.
- Meditate on forgiveness from the Word of God daily.

Chapter Eleven:
. . . .

Holiness

...Be ye holy; for I am holy.[1]

God is holy, and anyone who desires a relationship with Him must have holiness as a standard. What then is holiness? Holiness simply means a departure from iniquity.[2] It is, therefore, living without sin. However, holiness does not necessarily merge with infallibility. It only entails the purity of mind that brings about a sense of rejecting evil thoughts and unholy conduct. Thus one may live a holy life while still be capable of erring. The difference between him and a sinner is that, for the sinner, sinning has become a way of life. It is only normal for him to commit sin. His conscience does not prick him because, as it were, he has ceased from having one. For a person who leads a holy life, his conscience is always alert. At any point that he errs, his conscience will prick him, and he will begin to have a strong feeling of remorse that steers him almost irresistibly into repentance and resumption of the normal course of holiness.

The first practical step into a life of holiness is a genuine desire for it. You need to seek God with inward purity. Having done that, God will create in you a pure heart. Thereafter, He sprinkles you with "pure water," and you become clean from all your filthiness. The Scriptures refer to the Word of God as pure water.[3] When we have become soaked with the Word of God, we develop hatred for sin and develop love for righteousness.

To remain in holiness, we must strive to engage our minds—not with filthy things but with things that are worthy of God's name. In this regard, Paul has provided a suitable recipe:

> Finally, brethren, whatever things are true, whatever things are honest, whatever things are just, whatever things are lovely, whatever things are of good report; if there be any praise, think on these things.[4]

As we think about that which is pure, we become pure. As we think about that which is holy, we become holy. As we think about our Lord Jesus continually, we gradually transform into His image and likeness. The reason is simple: we change into the likeness of the object on which our gaze is fixed.

Our intention always must be honest. Consequently, we must avoid conspiracy or any plan to harm—no matter who is involved—or to obstruct, double-cross, discourage, blackmail, or even prevent anyone from attaining his desired goal in life. Like God, always think and desire good for others.

Holiness also entails respect for constituted authorities. Christians must therefore respect the law, for it would be a terrible thing for a Christian to be among lawbreakers.

Holiness must be reflected in our dress sense. This means that our dressing should promptly announce our identity as Christians. We must be careful not to identify with the congregation of the wicked by our mode of dressing.

In addition, our holiness must be reflected in our communication. We must reject the temptation to employ indecent language. We must be good examples for others to follow, even by our choice of words.

Holiness has a necessary relationship with forgiveness. You may never be able to live a life of holiness when you harbour resentment. Your mind must be free from all form of unwanted spiritual indebtedness. If you truly desire holiness, then you must be able to forgive all those who have offended you and to develop an inner feeling of love for everyone.

Holiness has a number of rewards. First, it makes you meet for the use of the Almighty God. To this extent, holiness opens the gate to anointing you for the work of God. Anointing puts you in a different class from your contemporaries:

> Thou has loved righteousness, and hated iniquity, therefore God,

even thy God hath anointed thee with the oil of gladness above thy fellows.[5]

Beyond this consideration, however, living a holy life brings you into union with God. Accordingly, He will never joke with you. Whatever bothers you also bothers Him. He will always respond to your request with a rushing attention.

For the eyes of the Lord are over the righteous and his ears are open unto their prayers: but the face of the Lord is against them that do evil.[5]

Holiness gives you access to revelation, which strengthens your faith and ultimately guarantees your destiny in Christ. The more we live in consecration, the quicker we receive revelation from the Holy Spirit of the mysteries of the kingdom of God.

Certainly, the last days have arrived, and we are about to witness the greatest move of the Spirit of God in church history. It will nevertheless require the purest men to take the lead. Are you going to be among their number?

Holiness is the basis for a perfect life. May we learn to live holy, moving toward godly perfection.

Tips that can help:

- Pray for the spirit of holiness in you.
- Make a decision today to live a holy life.
- Begin to let go of unprofitable habits, from the small and insignificant to the deadly and pronounced.
- Make a list of unprofitable habits you wish to work on this year.

Chapter Twelve:
. . . .

Sacrifice

For God so loved the world that he gave his only begotten Son, that whosoever believeth in him should not perish but have eternal life.[1]

A sense of sacrifice is a necessary foundation for personal relationships. It is all the more important when desiring a strong personal relationship with God. Sacrifice is self-denial. It is the feeling that prompts us into giving without any expectations for reward. To make sacrifice is to show consideration, feeling for our fellows, and commitment. Sacrifice is an enviable virtue for all true and faithful Christians.

Developing a sacrificial attitude to life requires that the individual must think less of himself and constantly watching out for what is pleasing to others. Although it may sound ridiculous, sacrifice involves making others feel better than we do. Frequently in our daily lives, we run into people who have nothing, while we have more than enough at our disposal. The spirit of giving is essential here. By sharing, we not only free ourselves from the vices of greed and avarice, but we also lessen the burden of need for others. Sharing is therefore one way of making the world one family. Being your brother's keeper starts with sharing. Such virtue should never cease. The reward is in the saying that givers never lack. This is a tested theory in human history and is phenomenally effective.

Sacrifice strengthens our consciousness and motivates our inner being to pursue the values of goodness. Love is the basis for a sacrificial attitude. If we lack love, we cannot make sacrifice. It is love for humanity that will move us to part with our material means for the benefit and comfort of others. Love for God will motivate us to make a quality sacrifice to God, whether in terms of our material possessions or our time and energy.

In making sacrifice, we need humility. In fact, we need humility to get close to others—especially to those who are less privileged than we are—and to create favorable conditions that will enhance the purpose for our interaction. When humility rules our attitude, we have a greater chance of approaching the level of those suffering around us—to understand their problems, appreciate their value, and be honestly committed to helping them out.

On the contrary, pride creates a wedge between us and our neighbours. Self-consciousness, which easily makes us develop a superiority complex over others simply because we are more privileged and fortunate, works against sacrificial spirit. Self-consciousness does not encourage giving or sharing. Pride thrives because of the obvious inequalities around us. No proud person will be genuinely committed to helping others, fighting their cause, or ensuring their happiness. Avoid discriminating against the lowly placed. Discrimination is wicked and evil. Withhold nothing from anyone when it is within your capacity to give.[2]

We need contentment and discipline to draw a line between what we want and what we really need. It is by discipline and contentment that we may truly show consideration for others. Consideration should always be for those who have nothing at all. This confirms our feeling of fellowship. Discipline dictates in us the values of moral conduct. It enables us to understand the social demands of society and to be guided by moral standards. Through discipline, we discover and appreciate the value of others. In particular, we appreciate that every person is useful, and no one is useless.

Sacrifice is both a social responsibility and spiritual duty. We commit ourselves to the survival of our society through our little sacrifices to individuals in need. Lack of communal progress and continuity brings stagnation and extinction. Those who fail to sacrifice for others are narrow-minded, selfish, and without vision. God, out of abundance of love, gave us Jesus Christ. He gave us His only begotten Son that we might through His death gain salvation. Thus, Jesus became the ransom sacrifice for our sins.

Sacrifice enables us to gain spiritual promotion. Jesus obtained a divine elevation. Upon resurrection, He became seated at the right hand of the Father, who has put all things under His power and authority. Sacrifice brought Solomon favour from the Lord. His sacrifice of a thousand bullocks provoked God into appearing to him in a dream and bringing him untold blessings. Abraham's willingness to sacrifice his son Isaac was the basis for God's immeasurable blessings for him. David was a man of sacrifice. He sacrificed everything within his reach: time, energy, resources, etc., for the pleasure of the Lord. In return, God established the throne of David, generation after generation. The widow of Zarephath sacrificed her family's last meal for Elijah, and God gave her more than enough for her family.[3]

The life of the Christian is a life of sacrifice. Learn to live sacrificially.

Tips that can help:

- Pray for the spirit of sacrifice in you.
- Resolve to live to make sacrifices every day.
- Identify a critical gap situation in humanity and begin to make contributions toward filling that gap.

Chapter Thirteen:
. . . .

Obedience

If ye be willing and obedient, ye shall eat the good of the land; But if ye refuse and rebel, ye shall be devoured with the sword: for the mouth of the Lord has spoken.[1]

The universe is hanging upon divine principles. In practice, these divine principles apply strictly to avoid collision. Obedience is therefore the first law of nature. God respects the principles and rules of nature as contained in His Word. No wonder He cannot allow His Word to fail or alter His covenant[2]. Anyone desiring to make progress in his walk with God must be willing and obedient. He must follow the rules, for God is no respecter of persons.[3] To succeed, a Christian must be ready to follow God's commandments as they are. He must practice them whether or not they are convenient to him.

What destroyed Saul was his thinking that he could substitute his own will for the will of God.[4] The sacrifice he had hoped to make to God was contrary to God's specific directive. He thus acted in disobedience and consequently paid for it with his kingdom. What a great lesson in obedience for us!

Jesus operated perfectly in obedience to the will of God. He willingly carried out God's directives in obedience. He surrendered even His life in obedience to God's will, and this earned Him the ultimate promotion.[5]

We must learn to be obedient to the will of God concerning us. We must be ready to follow His instructions on particular issues. However, there is no way we can ascertain the will of God if we cannot settle down to His Word. We must sincerely desire the Word of God. Moreover, we must develop the habit of withdrawing occasionally from the hustle of the world to seek the face of the Lord.[6] We should meditate always on His Word.[7]

Getting God's attention through His Word requires that we develop a mind-set that is distinct from the world. We must acknowledge that the world is passing away along with its desires. Our focus should be on the world to come rather than on this darksome world.

When we can focus steadily on God, we begin to understand His will. If we can follow the will of God as it is, then we are positioning ourselves for the good of the land.

The Psalmist explains the reward for obedience as follows:
…Blessed is the man that feareth the Lord that delighteth
greatly in His commandments. His seed shall be mighty
upon earth: the generation of the upright shall be blessed.
Wealth and riches shall be in his house: and his righteousness
endureth for ever.[8]

Tips that can help:

- Pray for the spirit of obedience.
- Resolve to live according to the will of God for your life.
- Understand the mind of God on every issue before you take any step in life.
- Never do a thing if it will not glorify God.
- Take every God-given assignment seriously.

Chapter Fourteen:
· · · · · · · · · · · · · ·

Power

God hath spoken once; twice have I heard this, that power belongeth unto God.[1]

The word power has different sheds of meanings. It can mean "the ability or right to control people or events" or "the right or authority to do something." Power is also the natural or special ability to do something.[2] For our purpose, however, we may define power as the ability to be in control of a situation or event. Power, therefore, equals dominion. Whatever you can control is under your dominion. Whatever you cannot control is beyond your power and therefore outside your dominion. The level of success attainable by any individual is a function of the extent of power he can exercise.

Power may be physical, spiritual, intellectual, economic, or political. Whatever nature it may assume, power is fundamental to life—although some forms of power are more fundamental than others. Physical power, or raw strength, is the least fundamental, while spiritual power is the ultimate. We have explained elsewhere in this book that man is a spirit that lives in the human body. Accordingly, his destiny is largely determined spiritually. If man it to attain good success in life, he must be able to wield spiritual influence. It is, however, a great impossibility to exercise power without being connected to the source of power. God is the ultimate source of all power. He is therefore in control of the entire universe.

God made man in His image and likeness. He put him in paradise and gave him dominion over the physical earth. Man actually exercised dominion until he surrendered it to the Devil through disobedience. The fall of man meant the loss of his dominion over the earth's physical environment. To put it mildly, man ceased from being in charge of his environment and, consequently, his destiny. This was how he began to live a precarious life at the mercy of the forces of nature. It took a skillful redemption programme and the release of power by God to recover dominion for man. The blood of Jesus Christ at the cross of Calvary sealed the redemption programme of God for man. Man lost perfection and needed a perfect sacrifice to return to perfection—a sacrifice only God could afford. With the death and resurrection of Jesus Christ, man recovered dominion.

However, mankind having lived for over six thousand years as spiritual slaves to the Devil, the new man hardly understands the dynamics of power. He has power but lacks the mentality to exercise it. As such, he continues to suffer all manner of limitations. He needs someone to explain the real situation to him; he needs to know that he is in control and not otherwise. This is the experience of most Christians today. Now hear it: you are born-again and redeemed. You belong to the church of God over which the gates of hell cannot prevail. In further assurance, Jesus said:

> Behold, I give unto you power to tread on serpents and scorpions, and over all the power of the enemy, and nothing shall by any means hurt you.[3]

This passage cannot be selective in its application. It does not relate specifically to the first-century Christians. Not at all. It applies to you and to every other Christian. How do I know? Because the Scriptures also say:

> But as many as received him, to them gave he the power to become The sons of God, even to them that believe on his name.[4]

Christians are outlets for the exercise of God's power and authority. A Christian who cannot conduct God's power is not living in dominion, and his experiences in the hands of the forces of wickedness can only be imagined. To be carriers of God's power, we must become consecrated. The Spirit of God is holy, hence it is addressed as the Holy Spirit. Paul was always conscious of himself as an oracle of God. At a certain level in his ministry, he became so full and intoxicated with the power of God that he declared:

And my speech and my preaching was not with enticing words
Of man's wisdom but in demonstration of the Spirit and of power.[5]

Paul could be so intoxicated with the Holy Spirit because he lived a life of purity. No wonder he exercised unlimited powers in the service of God. He was so convinced that purity would bring a Christian into the realm of limitless power that he counseled:

Having therefore these promises, dearly beloved, let us cleanse Ourselves from all filthiness of the flesh and spirit, perfecting holiness in the fear of God.[6]

Power is the ultimate for success. It is your right as a Christian to exercise power. The basis for the exercise of kingdom power is knowledge of God. Go for it.

Tips that can help:

- Understand that you are a replica of God.
- Convince yourself that you are born to exercise power.
- Search the Scriptures daily for power-packed words and use them.
- Exercise power on a daily basis by speaking to your circumstances.

Chapter Fifteen:
· · · · · · · · · · · · · ·

Joy

Thou wilt shew me the path of life; in your presence is fullness of joy; at thy right hand there are pleasures for evermore.[1]

Joy is a state of great happiness and pleasure.[2] It is the absence of sorrow and, therefore, evidence of the presence of God. A Christian who cannot experience joy is probably no longer standing right with God.

We noted elsewhere in this book that God sometimes allows His children to feel pain. This may bring about sorrow for the Christian. However, he is expected not to accommodate the sorrow. Instead, he should look up to God for strength. God will surely strengthen you with His joy.[3]

Joy is among the fruit of the Holy Spirit.[4] In other words, the Holy Spirit in the life of the Christian bears fruit, and one of them is joy.

The kingdom of God is a bundle of righteousness, peace, and joy in the Holy Ghost.[5] A Christian who experiences the joy of the Lord is already getting a feel of the kingdom of God while on earth.

The opposite of joy is sorrow. Sorrow is an indication of disconnection from the presence of God. Take another look at the anchor Scripture, and you will discover that there is no moment of grief with God. In our imitation of God, we must strive to avoid fits of anger. While we may have occasion to be angry sometimes, we must try to avoid remaining angry for a long time. Also, we may experience pain that arises from the sudden loss of a valuable or close relation or associate. However, the joy of the Lord must be our strength. When we constantly come into the presence of God, we contact the oil of gladness that heals our emotional wounds and restores us to a state of joyfulness.

May you continue to enjoy the kingdom of God as you constantly remain in the presence of the ever-loving Father.

Tips that can help:

- Pray for the spirit of gladness.
- Avoid associations that can dampen or destroy your joy.
- Attend Christian meetings regularly and punctually.
- Always be in the mood of praise.

Chapter Sixteen:

. . . .

Grace

As every man hath received the gift, even so minister the same one to another, as good stewards of the manifold grace of God.[1]

Grace or favour is divine enablement or help from above. It is God's kindness shown to man. Grace is an important attribute of God. A Christian desiring to exploit grace in his spiritual life must attract it and operate in it. Usually, grace is unmerited, but unusual grace can be provoked.

As Christians, we have a God-advantage. We have received the grace of God, and we need not labour unduly to attain success in life. The grace of God is freely available to all, but it abounds more with Christians. When we live a committed Christian life, we have assurance from the Word of God that whatsoever we do shall prosper.[2] Besides, we have an idea that in the end times, the church of Jesus Christ will command unusual favour.[3] Our God is a very gracious God.

Man lost his perfection and, by extension, eternity through disobedience. He therefore came under the influence of sin and death. When it pleased God, however, He arranged to redeem man. He decided to bring help to the helpless man. Thus, we are saved by His grace, justified by His grace, and made strong by His grace.[4]

Grace is vital, not just for salvation but also in lifting and empowering us. God is in the business of saving, lifting, and empowering people. His secret agenda lies in the expansion of His kingdom:

…My cities through prosperity shall yet be spread abroad …[5]

As Christians, we must endeavour to cultivate grace. We must show favour to others, always willing to make ourselves available as instruments for the uplifting of others. Our lives will not glorify God if we can hardly count those we have helped. Indeed, a quick method of provoking God's favour for upliftment is by showing favour to others—especially the less-privileged. Except we show favour, we are not yet candidates for divine promotion. When we give help, we also receive help. No wonder it is written:

Give and it shall be given unto you; good measure, pressed down, and shaken together, and running over, shall men give into your bosom.[6]

Stinginess is an anti-Christian character. In reality, it makes no sense. If anything, it is the opposite of graciousness and does not guarantee increase. Hence, the scriptures testify:

There is that scattereth and yet increaseth, and there is that withholdeth more than is meet but it tendeth to poverty.[7]

When we render help, we show that we are one with God. God is always helping us, even while we are ignorant of His grace. His grace is available also to the wicked, even unto salvation. Our show of favour should therefore not discriminate against those outside the household of faith. While giving priority to our brethren, we should also extend favours to unbelievers. Perchance we may help to convert them simply by rendering help to them.

We may render help using our talent, time, resources, and even our contacts. Regardless of the form of favour, we must endeavour to share whatever we have with others. Remember always that we are nothing and have nothing except by the grace of God.

Tips that can help:

- Pray for divine grace.
- See it as a privilege to be considered by God as an instrument for blessing someone.
- Identify at least one area of need in your environment or local church, and assist as much as you can to bring solution.

Conclusion

· · · · · · · · · ·

In this book, I have tried to explain Christian character as the Christian's moral behavioral pattern that is consistent with God's nature as exemplified in the life of Jesus Christ and revealed by the Holy Scriptures. I have also attempted to identify and articulate for the benefit of the reader some basic attributes of God, which every Christian must endeavour to cultivate.

While it is understood that at new birth every Christian will feel the bountiful love of God, I have an idea that only the Christian who has taken steps to perfect his Christianity can truly exercise kingdom power and authority. Perfection of Christianity becomes evident in the ease with which the Christian can reflect godly attributes.

The Christian who fails to perfect his Christianity has everything to lose. Invariably, he will need to contend with the challenges of living an earthly life. His ability to exercise kingdom power and authority will make him reign in the midst of life-threatening challenges. Conversely, his inability to exercise kingdom power and authority means he must operate subject to all manner of limitations. Christian character is therefore invaluable for every Christian.

If you desire to cultivate godly attributes, then you must be prepared to spend quality time with God. You will not only need to identify godly attributes, some of which have been articulated and presented in this book, but also to meditate constantly on them.

There is nothing like being at ease with the issues of life. God has created you to fill a vacuum. All that you need is to develop a deep personal relationship with Him, and He will guide you toward unlocking the great potential that is in you. This is my message in this book.

I have personally confirmed that no one has ever maintained a deep personal relationship with God and failed to dominate his generation. Your case will not be different, for God has never changed and will not change tomorrow.

Friend, I welcome you today to a higher realm of the supernatural and to the understanding of the ways of the Master.

References
. . . .

Introduction
. . . .

1. 2 Peter 1:3–4
2. Oxford Advanced Learners Dictionary
3. 2 Peter 1:4
4. 1 Peter 1:16
5. Matthew 5:13–16
6. Galatians 5:19–20
7. Genesis 11:6
8. Eluma Onyuike, Fil: Fundamentals of Moral Education (1995, unpublished).
9. Ibid.
10. Romans 12:2
11. Romans 8:6
12. Romans 12:2
13. Psalm 82:6

Chapter One
. . . .

1. 1 Peter 5:6
2. Isaiah 14:12
3. John 14:10
4. Philippians 2:5–7
5. Philippians 2:8
6. Isaiah 14:12

7. Philippians 2:9–11
8. Philippians 3:3
9. Philippians 3:7–10
10. 2 Corinthians 4:17

Chapter Two
. . . .
1. Ephesians 3:17–19
2. John 17:3
3. John 17:1–26
4. 4 Philippians 3:7–10
5. Proverbs 4:23
6. John 15:12
7. John 15:12–13
8. 2 Peter 3:9
9. Wikipedia, the Free Encyclopedia: "Christian Theology of Love"
10. Job 13:15
11. Hebrews 5:8–9
12. Ecclesiastes 7:14
13. James 1:2–4

Chapter Three
. . . .
1. Mark 11:22–23
2. Romans 12:3
3. Hebrews 11:1
4. Hebrews 11:6
5. Mark 9:23
6. Romans 10:17
7. Psalm 105:17–22
8. James 2:14
9. James 1:12

Chapter Four
. . . .
1. 2 Peter 3:9
2. Exodus 33:18–12 Peter 3:9
3. Isaiah 53:7

4. Hebrews 5:8–9

Chapter Five
· · · · · · · · · · · · · · · · · · · ·

1. John 17:17
2. This was the lifelong lamentation of Martin Heidegger, the German philosopher and proponent of the need for fundamental ontology.
3. James 1:18
4. John 14:6
5. Acts 5:1–11
6. Matthew 6:37
7. Psalm 34:11 Peter 3:10

Chapter Six
· · · · · · · · · · · · · · · · · · · ·

1. Matthew 12:35
2. Galatians 6:7
3. James 1:17
4. 1 Peter 3:13
5. Colossians 1:10

Chapter Seven
· · · · · · · · · · · · · · · · · · · ·

1. John 14:27
2. Psalm 19:1–2
3. 1 Kings 19:12
4. Isaiah 30:21
5. Proverbs 18:1
6. Isaiah 43:2
7. Isaiah 41:10
8. Exodus 14:14
9. Colossians 3:16

Chapter Eight
· · · · · · · · · · · · · · · · · · · ·

1. Proverbs 28:1
2. Revelation 5:6
3. Colossians 2:15

4. Revelation 1:6
5. 2 Timothy 1:7
6. Ephesians 2:6
7. 1 Peter 5:8
8. John 14:26

Chapter Nine
· ·
1. 1 Thessalonians 5:18
2. Romans 8:28
3. 1 Samuel 15:23
4. Romans 4:17
5. John 11:41

Chapter Ten
· ·
1. 1 John 1:9
2. 1 John 3:15

Chapter Eleven
· ·
1. 1 Peter 1:16
2. 2 Timothy 2:9
3. Ephesians 5:26; Hebrews 10:22
4. Philippians 4:8
5. Hebrews 1:9
6. 1 Peter 3:1Psalm 34:15

Chapter Twelve
· ·
1. John 3:16
2. Proverbs 3:27
3. 1 Kings 17

Chapter Thirteen
· ·
1. Isaiah 1:19–20
2. Psalm 89:34
3. Romans 2:11

4. 1 Samuel 15:22
5. Philippians 2:5–9
6. Proverbs 18:1
7. Joshua 1:8
8. Psalm 112:3

Chapter Fourteen
· ·

1. Psalm 62:11
2. Oxford Advanced Learners Dictionary
3. Luke 10:19
4. John 1:12
5. 1 Corinthians 2:4
6. 2 Corinthians 7:1

Chapter Fifteen
· ·

1. Psalm 16:11
2. Oxford Advanced Learners Dictionary
3. Nehemiah 8:10
4. Galatians 2:20

Chapter Sixteen
· ·

1. 1 Peter 4:10
2. Psalm 1:1–3; Joshua 1:8
3. Joel 2:28
4. Ephesians 2:4–9
5. Zechariah 1:17
6. Luke 6:38
7. Proverbs 11:24

About the Author

· · · · · · · · · · · · · · ·

An ordained teacher of the gospel, with messages for Christians in all nations, Sam Chukwuka Onyeka holds LL.B and LL.M degrees from Abia State University, Uturu (Nigeria), and MBA in Insurance and Risk Management from Enugu State University, Enugu (Nigeria). He is also Fellow of the Insurance Institute of Nigeria. He is currently employed by the Insurance Commission of Nigeria and doubles as Adjunct Lecturer in Law at Imo State University, Owerri (Nigeria). He has to his credit over a dozen books in various disciplines. His goal is to become an accomplished international evangelist.

About the Book
. . . .

This book is designed to challenge old and new Christians alike into a desire for higher levels of Christian experience. As a practical guide to living God's kind of life, it spotlights some deep attributes of God as reflected by the life of Jesus Christ and revealed in the Holy Scriptures.